MW01044649

Lucy 72

Lucy 72

RONALDO V. WILSON

1913

© 1913 PRESS
WWW.1913PRESS.ORG
1913PRESS@GMAIL.COM

LUCY 72 © 2018

1913 IS A NOT-FOR-PROFIT COLLECTIVE. CONTRIBUTIONS TO 1913 PRESS MAY BE TAX-DEDUCTIBLE.

MANUFACTURED IN THE OLDEST COUNTRY IN THE WORLD, THE UNITED STATES OF AMERICA.

MANY THANKS TO ALL THE ARTISTS, FROM THIS CENTURY AND THE LAST,
WHO MADE THIS PROJECT POSSIBLE.

FOUNDER & EDITRICE: SANDRA DOLLER
VICE-EDITOR & DESIGNER: BEN DOLLER
SOCIAL MEDIA EDITRIX: LESLIE PATRON
EDITRIXES-AT-LARGE: BISWAMIT DWIBEDY, BRIANNA JOHNSON, EMILY MERNIN

FRONT COVER: WILSON, RONALDO V. *BOMBSHELL*. 2015. ARTIST'S COLLECTION. SANTA CRUZ, CA.
WATER SOLUBLE OIL PASTELS AND INK ON PAPER (SKETCHBOOK), 162 X 225 MM.:
WILSON, RONALDO V. *OUR GIRL*. 2015. (DETAIL) ARTIST'S COLLECTION. SANTA CRUZ, CA. WATER SOLUBLE
OIL PASTELS AND INK ON PAPER (SKETCHBOOK), 162 X 225 MM.

BACK COVER: WILSON, RONALDO V. *OUR GIRL*. 2015. ARTIST'S COLLECTION. SANTA CRUZ, CA. WATER
SOLUBLE OIL PASTELS AND INK ON PAPER (SKETCHBOOK), 162 X 225 MM.

ISBN: 9780999004944

Contents

Lucy 72

1. LUCY BEGINS TO SPEAK

One ear is stuffed with Styrofoam, the other open in air.
The car floats up a hill, but in my head, heat rings.

Birds collect outside a room. A tic folds in the split tree.
When will I decide my wool skirt is too small for my hips?

I slipped down a flight, or was I gliding on a moving sidewalk,
or was I falling down a gorge?

There are no waterfalls in my dreams, only the strangeness of a family,
being strange with one another. One member wipes a table down.

The table is black. The family is black. I'm not, but I dreamt about them.
One was driving another to work. It was 6:30 in the morning.

A boy was being mean to his sister. Maybe after a fight: "Are you mad?"
I saw her, curly haired, in a sweater vest jammed to the steering wheel.

My name is Lucy. I am small and thin. What he feels is close to speaking.
I do not speak, unless I have to.

I am forever white, which means I am forever sealed. I don't feel entitled.
I feel more or less, normal.

When I think about being, I don't think about being white. These black people
—a sister and a brother—my dream family—are beautiful.

I want at least to believe so. I am beautiful, not by default, but by the nature
of what exists. My story is not long, and in it, there is a river.

A river in my head that spills over rocks: When my hair, left in a shower or in a pool,
or in anyone else's mouth, the thought occurs: a sister, fabric in a car.

2. LUCY EMBODIES HER OWN PRACTICE

If I lean slightly forward, my lower back won't hurt. There's no-one around, not even myself, because I've decided to ignore my own arms.

When that Black called me "Whitey" in the street, or when I thought he said this, my hair was shield enough against the encounter.

The name caller manifests from within a dream. He could have been lying.
Maybe he was too smart to throw a brick. I've read about the brick throwing.

I read about one, homeless, picking up a piece of a building and breaking it on a blonde, who was unfortunate to be moving down that street. But still, we rise.

We survive. When he yelled "Whitey," at me, I thought he yelled, "Beauty," Not "Sexy," "Bitch," not "Mommy," nor "Lover," "Ho" or "Honey."

Does he have a face? Am I as temporary? In the mirror, I want to ask, "Is that me?"
Is that the person he sees? My own beauty, I realize, is connected to his naming.

That uncontrollable speech that emerges, rotating around the edge of manner—such activity, as he clears his throat is mine.

I am rounder than round, skin wound around flesh and a mane of grey. I am nearly as white as the two horses at the top of the hill, who, if given fright, may attack.

My time is succinct, my curler, a fragment, fly-backs shifting in feathers.
I brood, my racing shoes slip away from my feet. I, burning sun,

I, pink face, particleboard smack up against the house—In the morning, I walk on the edge of a spring, veins shooting from the soil.

3. LUCY AND REGRET

In the hour, when my wine has begun to melt, I feel loss.
What self have I undone to become?

After my body fell out of a puddle of water, I thought I'd care. Of course, I would not,
nor could I care less. I told someone about my existence. She was black.

I'm not certain how I came up, or why, or how I would feel in a room full of others who did
not look like me, or who were me, but I realized that I looked into my hand and saw.

I saw the sea, a river with a hole in it, stairs that lead into a lake, a river below that, and then
inside of that chasm, a parapet, then a rim around my head.

Tonight, I looked at my shadow. I never really thought about it before. In my swim cap,
what was I but a pull of currents against my form?

If I thought about it, hard enough, what would motivate me to stop turning inside of myself,
to stop looking for the point where my whiteness begins?

My urgent hair breaking near the edge of forest, the whole of my face cracking into pieces as
I shift. What body do I own, gesturing?

Imagine, an image where the body slips outside of the frame of the self, one where I think
less about being a runner, and more about running, becoming even less.

What gores back into me is only the space of my body, drilling against my life—
I am made up, but if someone were to walk up on me—

4. LUCY IN THE MORNING

I have to eat. The eggs in Montreal, no matter how hard I asked for them to be poached, hard, someone in the kitchen makes them soft.

I've since decided to give up on eggs, save scrambled. Too, I like my bacon crisp.
I like my toast crunchy. And at lunch, I need chips.

I respond to my need for hardness as a matter of consequence. I'm not sure how this is connected to my identity, or if it has anything to do with last night's dream.

There were rows of stables underwater. I was submerged within them. Who was I in my water dream, in my weightlessness? What mattered was that I could breathe.

Today, I am eating eggs that are perfect, shiny in their hardness, and toast that is also right.
A version of me is eating a plate of eggs.

This surface is where the dream embeds, a flat place where upon which fits my hope about what I perceive as race.

I thought I saw stars the other day, but I realize there are no stars, only the sound of my cheeks and the skin around my eyes wrinkling.

A sculptor just told me that the brain and the hand are connected to one another with immeasurable speed. I believe him.

I believe him because he did not smell like he did during the day when we last ate together.
A part of me would like him, if he did not stink of work.

5. LUCY TELLS

I have no biography. I did not come from anyone, or out of a body.
I am an idea, or at least a recognizable thought connected to an event.

I can be a fact, stranded. My existence—white lady—in particular is driven by gesture.
It's as though I am in a cycle, stuck behind the dryer door.

My hair, which in the morning is jet red—at least that's how I imagine it—is connected
to gravity, so that if I peek out, it swings freely in a wash of radiance.

"She's pretty," is what people say behind my back, especially in the morning,
when my gait is not connected to my weight. I will never "work it," or get fat.

What I am is one small flash out of a window for a sec, say in a city, to check
the weather. I understand, in this timeline, I am safe.

What would it be like if I were black? What would I do or feel, leaning outside of a door?
Would the wind drive in various directions against my face?

There are so many versions of me I see: round, chaired, big-haired, bleached, glasses,
khaki-cropped, lo-jeaned, naked, biked, fanny-packed.

But if I were alone, surrounded by concrete bricks that had gaps, light, grey, ready to defy
their use, would I fret?

If I were only a maze, or a field of wildflowers struggling to fill the air—would I hinge
where I no longer imagine as I turn, shuffle in focus.

In a dream I had, I saw tunnels, but did not walk into any of them. What do I embody as
I flick my imaginary hair to one side?

What do I care of the diver discovered, preserved, at the bottom of the freezing lake—
"what age was she?"—and what age am I who has no start?

6. LUCY AT THE CENTER OF THE UNIVERSE

Though I have no start, I know where I began. It was underground, or in an elevator.
No skin. No blood.

I know I did not begin on a table. I was not prodded, nor dragged from the edges
of a dream, and I was created alert, fast.

Like a baby shark, flitting out of its mother, born ready to kill. Or like a turtle, nail
cutting its way out of the egg, only after absorbing all the fluid in the sack.

What surrounded me in the elevator was air, which was not exactly like falling
through the house. When I burned, cindering its floors, my body slipped down too.

I obliterated the carpet, burning through the hole of the moment I estimate as my birth.
The knocking at my door has nothing to do with me.

It's a sound that does not make me think about any noise besides the tone in which I live.
Did you think, for any minute, that I was less?

When I walk, people don't necessarily move out of the way, but I think they should.
I wonder what it'd be like to be so gigantic. In the big picture of things, I'm an event

at every corner. I'm more than a butterfly afloat. To the thought, I wipe my fingers,
and point, "but you said, you said!"

7. LUCY IS WHITE

My freedom is not white. Though my body is, I think, peach,
the color of what might be the insides of some animals.

There's melanin in me, deep in my fingers, the digits held not by shadow,
but like in my calves, darker, in summer, like in my house, erect.

In this, I am alive. Even at the risk of cancer, I step out in the sun. Even after flesh
cut and a mole pulled out, even after the tests, the results, I can only imagine tan.

In the sun, I am reminded I am human, that my body is whole. I am free to break
near the edge of whatever it is I want, say, to notice bikes collecting at a door.

Knowing is becoming the source, a familiar sign, not my peering out of a bush.
And I will not wash a dish.

In fact, I refuse to wait near any obligation, because I might leap off and dive
into a psychic grid of that which is familiar. I am blank, clear. I am pure, tested.

Last night, near the edge of a sea, there I was, lying yet arched up into the moon,
which looked heavy against the sky. It was yellow and cut the fog.

Or clouds. Like the hole in the needle in the haystack, I fit in, but I will not jump
from a hay bail. I do not think that I work like that.

Above me a roof, where water slides down, but I have no nation. I have no feeling
for boundary beyond my own.

I am playing a game. Can you guess it? My knees are bent and I pull something back.
It is winding backwards, wrapping around me.

8. LUCY RESPONDS TO MOTION AND REFLECTION

When the NORTH COUNTRY LINEN SERVICE backs its truck below my window, blaring Faith,
the thunder outside no longer matters.

The towels wave in front of my window. I can see them flying by the white skin
of the driver, who I want.

What I love is that he could care less about the music that disrupts my writing.
He could care less about the blare of my fan, or the thunder as he throws towels.

Each one reminds me I am surrounded by whiteness, that my real body is not white,
and my mind longs for something outside of its sanctity.

This reveals itself in the white streaks that gather at the edges of my skull,
the features of my face, above my laptop which my hair covers.

I've decided to feel invisible for the day, to ignore the great back muscle that rips down
his back. I'm not here to think about that.

I'm here to leave a message, to deliver myself from my reflection, shadow and force.
What I did not capture is a flash near the water.

The rain stopped. I recognized a pair of jeans on a line. I don't question my looking
at the white paint on the house railing.

If I am taller, or thinner, or finer—If I am more wealthy than the next—If I can recline
or walk along a beach, surf or run, or sew—or if I have an important name.

I want to devoid myself of all but jaw, apple, and glance. For my need: linens, hurled
bag after bag into the big truck, he carries a single blue one back.

9. LUCY AND REDEMPTION

In another part of my being, I thought about what the bag meant. I couldn't think of it without the hurling motion of towels that flew by.

I felt that what contained my own whiteness was being a body not black. It's like I'm in a black people movie, when I stuff my face. You know, all fried food.

I am white, pure as the matter of paint that I painted at the borders of my room, pure as the coatings that lay thick on my walls.

One of my favorite words is *alabaster*. It suits me in the winter, when my blush lights up a room, the glasses stop their clinking, and I become less cold.

I hope that my sense is tied to my actions. If I address a black face with a smile, what will that face do? If I presuppose his or her color stable, will I rotate or fade?

I cannot lie. I'm not sure what I want from this existence. If only I were more real, instead of less brimming at the surface.

The feeling is like a film in the back of my mind. There's race. There's gender. There is my skin, decision and circumstance, which I hope to peel.

There is the real peeling that I pick from my back. I can't wait to run or to swim. No objects that I can see for any real sense of duration. The landscape shifts.

I concoct one sense of my self in one way, and then another way until I have no race. Really? Is my whiteness connected to a past beyond its own right?

When my body spins in the morning, I give it power. When I enter a room to sit down with such alert intelligence, of course, I have such stunning bones and hair.

My fork is not a weapon. At times, I think about spitting in people's faces, right while they are speaking to me. The spit flies from my mind, again and again.

10. LUCY AND VIOLETS

Behind my head, there's a soft, vast field. The matter of this grows thick from veins
fed from rain and run off.

A part of me sits alone, waiting to hear the forest. How can I get out of feeling?
It's not guilt. I've said it so many times. I'm not afraid of being white.

I'm proud to be who I am, even though I share the name with that short woman—
Lucy, row of bones, I remember looking at her remains in books,

always fixed to the ruler that pinned her height so exactly.
I remember thinking *my length means nothing*.

Do I begin there? I think so much of how I wait near the edge of my own being.
The flowers collapse into the world beneath us both.

Were I to bend my back all the way back, look dreamily up into the sky then the land
behind me, would I submerge my thoughts, still shooting back?

I consent to not ever feeling. It's easier that way. It's easier for me to look into a mirror
and to see my hair as simply a device, my eyes as a plan beyond seeing.

"Lucy, she has the prettiest eyes. I think they're violet." One eye is like a cat's.
It's what gives me my power, the way the iris is slit, a bright line.

II. LUCY SEES ANOTHER SIGN

The bug's zigzag could mean the end of its life, or that it cast a shell,
or maybe it was simply excited to be alive.

But of course, the bug hadn't thought about living, no more than the duck
outside my window in a pond is stuck.

To project loss—as if the exoskeleton around one body is like feathers around,
or the fat in another. Though I know I can't eat, I know they do.

Hunger is wound around nothing but air, angle and light.
My focus, a shadow bound by a stain, to which a feather is gummed.

I've walked along tracks. But I've never felt such fear,
stepping from plank to plank.

Leaping between wood with as much speed, sometimes
my body gives up. Sometimes I don't have one.

I've learned to abandon who I am in favor of my intention,
which is why I identify with the white in gesso or eggs, ice or clouds.

12. LUCY: SEEING MYSELF

What's easiest for me is being able to look into faces that don't care.
What shoots from their eyes, brains that flip, emit.

The realization is tied to what makes me beautiful.
If I see my body as one surface, and feel my gut, I think I'm full.

Will I be alert enough to guide myself along the chasm of what I do,
to not reject my hair, tired and heavy from the day?

A bee mistook my do for a field of flowers, and chased,
made its way to my face. I felt it needed to sting.

It's not that I wasn't uncomfortable with this fact. I just feel soured
by how I interact with others. I feel dark. Just saying.

Sleepy against a wall, I fragment against a mirror, sweating.
When the rain stops, I'm less threatened by my drift—To be social

my elbow doesn't fold much, nor does my heart. I will not avoid my chin,
sharp against the ledge. The sun rolls around the edge,

like the bulb hopes to spark, or to vaporize substance. Here, I expire—
No, I don't. I carry a rock, stick or gun. I kick, punch, stab and force.

13. LUCY, THE RAIN

When it starts and the pavement turns black, you will see me looking
for difference between what's dry and what shines.

Wetter than wet, beyond black, my whiteness is like my voice,
a melody of sunflowers bleached and dried in a closet.

I've never heard my voice beyond what I can only intuit—it sounds
girl enough for one to want to possess it, boy enough to trump the rain.

Sometimes, when it comes down, the drops crash on the pavement,
little explosions, the clarity of my speech.

I do not stutter, or vary my pitch. I do not smoke, or drink more than red.
Cropped pants: the sun runs. The field of flowers that grew,

I have picked clear. Next to a sea, I saw a pair of eyes, almost blue-green,
after which I lay out before the storm to rest.

Against my arm, a silver chair, and if I had a song to sing, it would begin
with my body, blocked. The day breaks out the darkening sky,

and when I wear black, I look even longer, my kick underneath even firmer,
they, too, say I light up a room, and they say, even my eyes are so clear.

14. LUCY ALMOST DROWNS

I did not think about my skin in the water. Its color didn't matter.
After all, I was a girl, caught in a tide pool.

Before I slipped in, I thought about place. Would I judge the black
that grew over the rocks? Could I peel back?

In that portrait, where I am only a black head suffocated by a white bag,
What self do I occupy?

Free. Dumb. In the water, I'm not exact. My arms push against my current,
face, gliding under, below where I see nothing.

My head splits on a rock before I throw my body forward to see
who I am. What black does not feel? What black does?

On the street, in a bank, in an alley, up a chair, in a tree, up the bark,
down a fall—No impulse, but to watch me in the water, circle.

15. LUCY AND BLACKNESS

I live out of where air shoots through the sky—
This pressure is what doubles me, and splits.

I think I have seen it all, like tonight, in a series of symbols,
for instance, one: a vessel in a grid.

And I think about the trees. I think I'm alive in that moment
when a branch bends into what it wants,

something sticky as the juice that wets my finger, like the scent
curled in the pocket of the squirrel burrowing.

I'm wrapped and tucked in a towel. A mask I wear at night—
it saves me from the sight of my own skin.

There is a sky, and there is a cloud. There is my body, out there,
I, of course am free. Is there any other way? I might get turned out.

I might go into the day to search. I might decide not to speak.
It's too easy to be empty—the body drills my song, *I am not black.*

16. LUCY LOOKS

Where the fan blows a red thread into the room—
It is where I think.

I can't wait to let myself speak, my eyes grown over with moss,
my sight, caught under a tree.

There is under this, a radiance that breaks open the day, dull buzz
against the heat of the afternoon against which I crouch.

Light sticks to the cloth and burns into the clutch of white
egg-specks on the green shirt I hung to dry.

My body in sonar, the shot of one word bounced from my face back
from the shirt to the black who is looking at my little mouth.

17. LUCY AND FREEDOM

If I think about my own unwinding, I can see my freedom
in relation to the bug flicked

in the street, its wings soft from dying in the envelope.
In the night, its color, then, against the white of my room,

bouncing against the walls, brown and quick. I'm not sure if
its kind matters, smacking against the ceiling, to escape hardness.

I thought about it charging my body, its speed, and ruining
the neon bulb. Tricky spinner, I thought the noise I could deal with,

but the point when I realized I was done, it fell in my bed.
It didn't want to be caught, but it had to be captured.

The towel worked. Snapped in the air, trapped in a grey cap
filled with foam—

Below the flap—more tape—sealed. I'm not sure why I decided
to bake it over the bulb, maybe because of all the scratching.

There is a body inside of a body. I did not think of that then,
but I think of it now.

18. LUCY AND LIFE

One last push against paper, trap, heat, and hate. I decide to release
you into the street, your wings baked into your back, and you wobble.

Did you fight as I wrestled in sleep? Did you rest in the envelope?
Think of death, scratching through the night? The bulb baking you,

into you, the unrest of one animal sounds like the squeak of cricket
or rat, then the smell of skunk hovers in my room.

I think my skin is too soft for killing, but my fingers remain hard
and hit like hammers.

Fog collects below the trees in the ropey air, and I wind in.
There are no shadows. No sound.

Insect, in fact, snagged from the earth, you will not fly,
wings seared, and still I want to crush your body. Pull you close.

Or pull your head off tonight. Small and alone in my whiteness—
the world is not bigger than my safety in it, and the river runs behind.

19. LUCY WAKES

The silt in my mind, shadows in the bushes,
but the water from the spring in the jug

gathers around light. I bloat. I'm cold in the night.
What have I eaten? Wind in my voice, breath in where

the force is overt: me, gravity, depth, hair. To be lost.
Fragments still float. The pieces circle,

collect, a billowing in the dirty water. To undo,
I swim, but the leech attached

to a star, unhinged—is sight—I have been here before,
awoken at the edges of gaps that grow

in the green moss under the water,
where my eyes flatten.

20. LUCY IS DROWNING IN SORROW

The duck has a story. It is black. Been mauled by dogs. This is its history—
the graph of its life trapped in an eddy,

the same whose insides haunt, who has decided to sing:
This is the edge of him, alive. And I surmise this is the edge of her,

living in a park that cuts off into a ditch where my body is slick:
What surface do you see when you pomade it down?

What hope do I have for the sore that grows from the roots? Wind holds
what I am, a curtain cord knots. The sun, flat on a sill,

pulls me to the light fragmenting on the pool's bottom. I skirt.
The winged draw of my blackness, currents, I suck in, and blow:

I think I'm alone now, becoming, dodging what clings to my own wall.
White knocks—I'm caught all up in it.

21. LUCY LOOKS UP AT THE GREAT SKY

Over there, above that field, a sky opens up into one patch that's grey.
I find that if I look away from all pavement to where the ground

is still black, worn between rock and grass, then I fixate
on a wire that cuts the horizon. I miss, too, being with the others.

The rain is a long sentence that spills, but doesn't free my time,
so why do I stare? What trap has been set to ask of me:

Did they really hang in trees, or crumple dead in palmetto scrubs,
bodies bulleted, obliterated?—And though some faces remain,

I pull up my skirt, walk through the forest, unbothered by the thought,
to here, where a gull shoots up the side of a rust-red cliff.

I mean to see one event, but it's hard to be near enough to another,
to recall a lake, or this water crashing. Is that force over there, a space

distraction enough to grind against? Lying on the bench, back then,
taking a breather. Now, plastic wrap my head, a body stripped, knees to chest.

22. LUCY'S TRUTH

What's coming from that stack of two-by-fours? I feel hogtied and shocked
into numbness. I can't erase the kind of black I am,

no face, only a body, wrapped and in the street,
or arms bound behind my back. The body cuffed by steel, or plastic,

both wrists held tight, the burnt end of a braid, a lotioned cheek.
What propels me is how I don't have to see that piece of meat in the store

as this black on the curb. The thought does not make me want to vomit.
I remain thin in my face, and the fan pushes the heavy air.

My hope, the pressure will reach where I want to go outside to run.
My body, under another sky in the day, will race up the impossible hill—

Is there anyone up there where the siren finds its hole? Being among you
is mostly a feeling where there's no visible net, and you're so bound.

On the pond, a film—I'm not sure if this is something that comes
from seeing the distance between my own body and his, roped up.

Today I saw another black: curly haired in crimps, large and round,
her hair thick, wound spirals. I got jealous. She was playing with a little white

boy on a unicycle. I don't feel strange about their positions. My mouth
cannot hold what it chews. It is my history, too, the piss that falls from between

my legs, that fills the grass and now soaks, and is also inside me. Roses curl up
above the other flowers, but above them all, my matte pink face.

23. IN LUCY

There are rays. At least they look like rays, though I'm not under the sun.
I feel it in me, the heat collecting in my remembering this:

If I burst, my body must bend. Reach North. Up here, I don't get a signal,
but if I did, my head would flood in the cell stream of my talking and talking

as if against what I force myself to say, or what it takes to not deal
with what I've left on the shower floor.

I slept on a thin bench. My body felt, for the first time in a while,
small and still—but what I saw after my nap, more doubling shadows:

I don't like the sky in the afternoon, because it isn't the fog,
only me in this space, only me, for sure, but to glance into the face

of a black I saw on the street, at night, with the trees dripping on us both,
and one more, there, a hiker. I drive up the hill, recalling them, in my turning.

24. LUCY'S PACE

I have seen myself in dreams, a tall black girl, walking, not ever aimless,
but with the gait of a stalker, pushing her body forward:

I have seen her force herself over grasses. The anger in me
coils against my back, gathers to push me from my empty bed.

I have seen her walk across sand, each grain loosening beneath her feet,
always catching her before she slips.

Even her figure trails me, ready to hunt down what I sense. She's not me.
I am as opaque as the fog cutting through the street lamps,

yellow by plane. I want to evaporate across this horizon—
as in the fear that takes hold as I sit with them, running in place, as ever

always escaping—what have I done to eat so little, to be so hot, so invisible
on one side, and on another, thick, my race—does it always lead me?

25. LUCY AND THE SUN

Of course, I don't fear it. I look up into its face and see myself.
The bright not melting or burning, but leading me into the shiny stone,

flat and red, striped with white streaks that flow on its top.
It doesn't overheat, more than it keeps me safe from my body, not bone,

but warm. A black wouldn't see me without a rack. Billiard balls nest
in a triangle, so am I soft in my heart? I wait where I was born,

I break, softly, as if lying on a plate. Shell, I'm not sure
I will ever be hard. Whites, I am raw. Even where my body cramps,

I wonder what it means to be half and half? I can feel the black coming.
I enter a code, pull myself through a tiny room, dart away, my sight.

26. LUCY IN A FORCE

A fog creeps up near the edge.
What was I thinking up on a hill

with the rain filling the sky in this white
body of mine spilling? I don't feel taint

beyond the arc, past the end of my face.
No wide nose. No naps. No real fat lips.

I'm getting close to absence now, ripping
away these mountains, I slip into this mist.

27. LUCY AND MOVEMENT

My body is full, while a black is a fragment.
I will not dream beyond texture, nor long for a sea;

instead, the field of grass thick as a substance
pulls itself out of the fire, holding the body alight

like a locket that forced itself open—the self,
shocked against the exit of the self?

In the opening, piles of leaves are not there
to shake and gather against my brain.

In the night they have left, and I'm all numb.
I, looking at a leaf, lying on a black surface,

I, pushing my speech forward as one act—
 the first slip of my own body into the night.

My motivation, the next, the whole of my back
arching forward, to reveal this:

There is my body, and there is his.
Two iron poles shoot dark and hard, some crust

formed between us, where the sea air gives way
to the red mountain trail, to the rip

of the brown tide. Feeling, and looking
out over the coast, knowing, *why is he so black?*

28. LUCY AS LYCIDAS

"Amarillo," is what I remember, and my body gone. I swirl, looking,
but what I want is to be left alone:

"Can Art Survive Death?" When I was asked to ponder this, my hand held
out so I could see it in the screen, flapping. I chased down the taupe moth

to a white wall, where I sit across the street and see, also the night ripped
open by rivulets where there's no visible river.

My feet, then, were black, moss fixed, near them on some craggy stone,
where trees spread into rays that shot

my breath full of specks. In a room, I look at a body, a green patch
on the neck. I don't think about the color of his skin, but the paint,

burnt black. If I were green, would I shine as much as I do now?
My skin radiates, as does my fear, beaming, but crammed.

I'm caught in an old Dunlop tennis racket with thick black string, filament:
I believed her, my black friend, when the white man slapped the cash

on the marble top, the shock, hit a bottom in my mind. Too, I felt something
gut. The white woman didn't sell me the newer fan, either, or the box.

29. LUCY, AGAIN, WITH LYCIDAS

I was thinking about the color yellow, amarillo,
like amarillys. Where the blade spins, I've no room.

I've no body to look at, no death to stare into,
nor trace of the shore, cast

in the shrub outside my window. Brown branches
twist through the picture, the memory of that body:

Postcards, I found myself—in one, she is white. Tangled
in my brain, I see her hands. Not drowning, lynched,

I'm hung. Posed for a picture with a man today.
The unnamed, a record, another useless map:

No rage sits in this grid. No edges catch,
no unmaking, not entranced, nor a finding left.

30. LUCY AND THE BLACK WHEELBARROW

If I ignore the fan pushing, still, my brain won't stop. I know my race is not more than an idea. I know, too, what it's like to resist the periphery of sight.

The way it peers around a figure that's made of porcelain, cracked, the dish, broken by the tiring stares, to repeat, again and again, what's clearly said.

That thought, or the smacking of the rain from the grey in the sky. Is it enough, to see such hard, black, living?

Is it like the great mouth of a whale, sucking in the krill, plant, fish or other, tailed? My head is lead by arteries that valve to my heart. The rubber tires spin.

Wheels grip the black asphalt. I take in the image of the body, carting it in, wheels flung off. My blues: a brown squirrel, striped, dipping in.

There's always the thought to which I've given over, where my mind spreads across the edge of broken. What hold do I have?

What holds me in as I think about what I know, but cannot? When I finally push and talk to you, there, against the edge of a chair, I eat.

Where I construct near a fall, the body loads up. What will I see in the fog, in the masses of mountains that grow into my sight?

Below, a black pond: I look into the water, flat against my window, a pouring down, the face of a statue being rained on.

Nothing comes from me, but the sound of the water leaving my eyes. Nothing comes out, not even the sweat I hold in.

If there's a hole inside of me, it's darker than black, so that the flesh I feel is open like the sky in my head, the flowing, as if water, gone to rush.

31. LUCY, WHERE

It's not in my vision where I see the trees breaking,
not this feeling of my body lost

in my breath which I keep stored in my throat.
I hope to release it across a field.

Where does the opening of a self drift?
I find it moving in the cross-draft

where the shadows sift up a hill, my stomach fills
there in the rain pool the wasps survive in.

To shield me from their hive, I listen to thunder
crack the sky, and later, the fog horn punching the air.

Now, in the opening of my face, a river splits my chest,
how can I make myself hate less and love more?

What path do I choose with my endless talking?
My mouth spins out: "This all came from my head."

32. LUCY IS HUNGRY

At night, the brown feasts on black asphalt. His mind,
is the street, where the pavement's cracked.

Twice, now, I looked at the street, so puzzled below me.
Who will fall before it's freshly filled?

How can I read the pain shooting up his back?
What can I say to the S'Mores I stuff in my face?

I want to eat forever. In the death of my diet, I'm stuck,
the trees burnt, too, in my dream, a hard crust.

Did he run over the bridge? Did he lurch back,
look at me? My breath thuds.

I lost the trail of my body to the caved hurt,
my tender, sunken head.

33. LUCY OPENS HER HEART

We've been cornered for so long, but I sense an end.
It shifts along the window's sill.

Light dances on the glass and leaves behind wind.
It drives the shadows on my house.

A breeze fights the fan that winds me up. What self
do I hear in the bark at the back of a porch?

A butterfly winds up, too, spirals to the tree top, mad,
up a ladder—wings in a dream I've not yet had.

Once I do, I see a little brown girl with a fat toy gun.
She stops a white man in a car, draws him out.

He pulls. Her gun is fake, his real. There's a black baby,
she takes aim to protect.

Too late, she remembers she has no bullets. She's shot.
Some black holds his sister stiff, bloodless—she dies,

frozen in his arms. And the bullet hole, too, is black
in a circle, dry and cold.

34. LUCY, AGAIN, OPENING

I wonder what it's like to be brown? In summer,
I lay in the sun until the heat numbs, *c'mon*,

Sand push back waves, blue open to green.
I'm all here, looking at the fish and nettles.

Sea alive with minnows—jet, long sheets confuse
the gull that spots one of us, slow, shallow, a picking

but I feel various, too, my eyes lap. The white sheet
rears up high and sinks. Plover, dot. Another screech—

This summer, the storms destroyed the coast, and the stairs:
Look, exposed bone. Short run of beach. No quiet stretch,

but the water, and its beat. I don't want it to crash,
but if it does, I won't see what's in front or what's behind.

35. LUCY, THE CONFINED

I refuse the black that eclipses my sight.
I see my hands, wiry; however, is my flesh granite?

Quartz cuts my pink skin,
and velvet is my head, now, what's rubbing on my face?

The spider's weave isn't, and as dense as the silk worm's
pocket catches, where these webs meet, I think about race

mapped in the drops on the screen, a water
line that blobs to the floor: can it be marked?

Some drops are perfect, some slide. Some are like glass—
see through—to the whisper of fans that sound, my world.

In my body, I point at the place on the apple before I bite.
Rot turned away, fresh skin on my teeth.

36. LUCY, IN A LINE

I imagine myself lying thin on one. My body, a string, stretched to the end of one pole
to another. My being—it's not who I am.

It's what it means when I lie between them. I'm not feeling the run yet, but I do feel
the strain of the thought, as I stretch.

To not resist myself, I tug. In fact, I might refract, depending on how I read my own
leaning into abstraction.

The black wants to spit across the small space between us, tells me: "you know, I want
to spit on your face," but he won't. He knows what it's like.

To be spit on in the face. The mind does not matter, nor does the labor of the act—
what does, is the smell of the spit when it sticks—despite rubbing a face in the grass.

Despite the brown patches that burn through the green openings, it's not color,
in the end, that matters.

Perhaps if I, as the white in my own mind, and in my own intention as a spitting body,
decide to release, then I'd lose my face.

I'd lose it, joyfully, if I could, the thought leapt like a lamb into a dream, or maybe it
plummets into some river, weighed down, into depth.

Damned, I stare at the surface. I feel the flood against my own ebbing, hear the clicks,
the fan gunning into the night-weight—smell the fat burn in the air.

If my body fell, there, crashing through the dark water's surface, my confessions to any
false lake wouldn't hold.

I, shaking, have no place to think about this dead end of meaning, as I am so important: What freedom do I want?

Part of me flies, white and tumbling through the air into part of you, wanting to release from your face to mine.

Are you so devoid, you can't imagine like me, looking out over the arc, unfurling in the substance that binds us, both, expelled?

37. LUCY BREAKS

In my head, a guitar loops: *"Snap a neck for some live effects!"*
How can I hear rap against the mountain where my knees give?

The trying in being all black—where you come from unravels,
in the wet morning, despite what chokes—why are you yelling?

Unraveling: who else with you screams up a hill?
"Maybe I'll shoot 'em now. Maybe I'll shoot 'em later!"

Why are you so noisy? That body of yours rots and is ugly,
or maybe, like the lung-fish, you're ready to soak back to fine.

The whisper of my voice in your throat as you push awake,
so high above me, to see a tree cut in the open light.

No, fog, I'm not to illuminate—I'm only the hill, sloping into the sky.
An old black body dropped in a vat of oil, boils, screams,

no, I don't need to listen to you. The light beats back in.
It's my breath. Or the sound of a cool down,

fan in my window, the forest is not silent, either, leaves
ground in by steps—this sound undone by *"Help! Help! Help!"*

38. LUCY RUNNING FROM WHITENESS

I did not guess the sign—in the night, someone forgot to flush.
What's left could be mine, but the cloud of toilet paper made me sick.

And the rain spits on the trails of where I scream to escape
from the three dogs that chase in a pack. You're haunted, aren't you?

By flesh, by the tone of your own voice,
you run back to the only person you see, miles down the road.

The stick in my hand swings across my body, accurate weapon,
as though I am a ballast for its spring and threat.

I leap over a dead frog, its skin, dry and smashed flat, amphibious
bones, I want to make up my hands. How will I escape looking back?

He's in front of me, far up the hill, walking deep into the forest,
pacing himself, slow and even through the hills. His hands, curved

and soft. Though his father is an oilman, he looks like a jock,
born and raised in the mountains.

Before, I thought he would be waiting for me, lurking in the high bush.
Maybe he'd have a gun, or a knife? Was the rock enough?

Was your speed in time with my song: "I Remember Lucy,"
and my speed, what can I say, but it saved me.

My voice, someone else's, an animal, growling, and you, lunatic,
screaming into the sky you see up in—*you look crazy.*

39. LUCY AND HER REALITY

In my dream, I am heavier than I am now, but remember, I am not white.
Muscle surrounds me, cuts into fiber and wraps around my bones

so close to memory, they too, bound so hard around my mind
which wants to fling, shot rubber band,

or crouching against trees, the grass returns. In the summer, my skin is dark,
but it's starting to get light—Fall's turn from opaque to clear.

You can see inside of me if I don't move, my body empty of shit and water,
and full of blood. In this body, I can't enter you.

Lately, your glances are lost in the light of the morning burning
where there's no distance between us, my face is still shellacked.

There are trees sunk below rivers. Some split boats. I can't know if my
skin is hard or soft, face blown smooth by wind, sealed by polymer and heat.

40. LUCY CONSUMES WITH INTENT

The tree beyond the screen is not flat, and through the green,
I make my sight blur in the metal grid.

It keeps out the gnats. A branch cradles up above the fat trunk
and the moss spots are thick in the sill of memory.

Blur, I'm not brown, nor do I glow, but a part of my want
is attached to my breath, which I hold close to the grass line

as if my arms reach out above the yellowing leaf. To suck light,
I hide beneath the grey bird that will drown if it nicks the sea.

A spider web weaves beneath the two cracks that arc,
like I don't have a belly? I'd rather not eat than be black.

The flamingos grow pink with algae. A black runs in a forest.
He's a male, 5'7", 176 lbs., and muscled.

To DAS EFX, he dances in the street. Or a black in my brain—
he does a typical jig, or imagines himself red as a college mascot,

dead self-tossed in the dryer. If I walk, am I lost in the auburn updo,
or if my hair's caught where I sink, will each bite bulge my lips?

41. LUCY IS NOT INSANE

In the crowd with the others, I don't feel strange. My hair is not brown
and cropped, my eyes not wide.

I am not shitting on myself, save lactose, I piss at the thought of being ripped
into oblivia. My legs are svelt, the muscle in them, solid.

It should be, from running in the tunnel of my own dreams, at night,
where there is no sun to shine.

If I had a name like Angel, I would stand out. I could wear less black at parties
I'd be an illusion. I cyclone, here, where my mind crops—

Sometimes my hair is pressed flat with an iron, red and flows down my back.
Sometimes I am short, and my whole face cataracts.

Sometimes, I am a screw driven into the stacks of lumber I saw while running.
My face breaks across a pile, I am a shadow in the cup.

In my mind, there is a shadow that shoots across my brain.
I think this is called flashing. I flash trucks that bounce down the street.

I am not sound, but it would be easy if I were, the hush of the cut in the tree.
Its white flesh might be the place where I am these questions:

She black? Is she, behind the window of the Saab with the tinted windows?
Am I that dark, even in the summer?

Well, last night, a skunk ran across the black street and I thought the world
would shift in the skin around my eyes.

42. LUCY'S COLOR

In the yellow mouth of the red bird is a red hole,
An opening that burns into a black

foam built where color suspends.
It's almost a kind of wish to pile up.

Bubbles collect near the surface of where I
break, as I look where I can't feel my breasts.

I push weight in the air to keep my lungs up,
the muscle below me, its broken down mass.

I run across a river. The body folds into a frame,
a blue plastic pot, a field, a white one on its side.

Often at night, I am the skunk traveling, white streaks
my back. I am real, and I am a present state.

43. LUCY SEES AGAIN

The man from NORTH COUNTRY LINEN SERVICE came again,
and the white towels fly across the arc of my screen.

Today, I swear, I looked at myself, walking down the road as I saw
two women who looked like me. One was thin and the back

of the other's legs were fat. Two streaks lined up the back of my own.
I thought about him spinning to safety as he pulled around the truck,

jumping off the back, twisting. I miss wanting him, the way he swung
out to break the plane of my vision. I saw him in the baldness of my desire,

my leaning out into the open air, shunned. Before he backed up, he threw
one towel aside. Is that the sign I am looking for?

There's another black in the town where I live. He wears a big red shirt.
He's a storm down the street, breaking into pieces as he bolts forward.

His walk makes a swoosh above the bridge he makes it across.
I try to ignore the rebar that climbs through the cement.

There's no figure in my own imagination as I run with my back,
hurling one white towel out of a room, and watching his fly from him

onto the truck bed. Why doesn't he look in? Might he know I am split between looking?
As I watched, I thought: all that loose cotton, all that waste of my time.

44. LUCY, LUCY, LUCY

How many of us have tails? When I asked him, about his, pliant bone coming
from below his seat, I realized that I'd said something about how it was steel.

Conductors float in the air, at night, above me, steel grids levitate over me, while I walk
below them. Actually, I forget the night.

I am dislocated beyond sense, my own body runs without my leaving it, over a field
that I've never seen before, but my legs are long and wiry.

They shock me into speed. A truck pounds against my imagination, the drum in what if
my language were so strange? What if what I said came as fast and loose from my lips?

I am not the house, nor am I the paint's color—such white, a bluing in the morning
against the fire lit last night.

I did not awake to dawn, or a hole in the earth, one that opened up the street to the sound
of a car whisking over it:

Why do I illuminate? Here, shadows play against my fingers, but in this light
I can only imagine running from him.

45. LUCY AT THE PRECIPICE

I am not alone. There are loons dying. I am not a loon, swimming against the current, chasing after what floats down the brown stream. I am beautiful, sitting, here.

The bench is hard and breaks my posture as I lean into what calls me. Is my hair such gold and fire? Is my heart such weight that it beats open my chest? There are mountains.

The trees above me, pull. *Wait there, near the edge of the light that breaks.*
In this broken, I seek the wind.

My hair needs to blow, bounce and shake like a shield in front of me, or maybe I need to bleach.

What must I unlearn to walk? What must I undo to leave for miles out where I am free, chasing after an opening. *I am.*

I am pulling myself out and up from where I sit, white girl on the rocks, black face lightening to shadows that shows my belly falling out into the street.

I am against a wall, pushing it back, my body, a force against walking. Of course, there is always my fear in moving forward.

What would I say, where? If I could say something else? Would I inscribe a language of my own design, force syllables through my throat, let them pour out?

In the shifting weight outside of the window, one black object. It is its face I want to look at, that shadow, its thick skin.

In a dark hour, my own self breaking into fragments that it breaks into. Can I leave my whiteness as it unloads such black?

What would I think, hovering there at the end of light, my exhaustion, turned over until the body's crook is left, a single point. Unmine.

Is there a hole in my head? Does it open to the edge of my belief in the trees? Does it gape, there, by the violent iron, eating at the columns of my own grief?

Or am I mis-feeling grief for exhaustion, looking out over the rush of white that fuels the water's push over the rocks.

When I return to it, as memory, holding it in, tight as I can, I squeeze what I see, open, until it snaps into sense.

46. LUCY SINGS

My cough is as dense as the trash that fills the basket, the waste I push
to the side of the road, far from the crows standing thick atop the branch.

I've left what I believe on the surface of the grass, underneath
where the wind cuts beneath the trees.

I am no danger. A bottle has fallen into the gutter,
stuck in the rusted grate. Water spouts out disappointment.

To this, I am singing, *Oh, Dear Lord.* I find the towels, white, stacked high,
left, near the light of the mist on the porch.

I am not surprised that people wave at me as I walk up into the sky
to meet the view.

I am not the horses, not the one that turns and begins to walk towards me,
but I am the sound of the water running below the side of the highway.

So vast is whiteness, my fear, a little, across the sign: FALLING ROCKS.
What if, no warning?

How could I walk, even further, down the road of my endless construction?
I've dreamed all my life, and once, in my glory, I was painted on a silver surface.

Even I, a pulse from somewhere else, attached to my fear of seeing another,
unlike me, matter like me, and connected by my knowing, *I got this.*

47. LUCY AND SHADOW

Leaves grow through porch slats, bursting from the broken steps,
the small stones I wish in my mouth.

I cannot speak, but when I have to, I hold in my throat, a soft light,
curving forward to the front of my palate.

Puddles beam through the air into my eyes. There's a pattern.
Evaporation, my mark fades on the cement.

In there lie my eyes, too, which vanish. My face blanks to nothing.
Nor does my nose matter. No. My eyes.

My teeth. No. The grass is thick with dew at night.
A truck is backing up, and I can hear it through the atmosphere.

Through the thicket of my projections, through the brown
of the broken pine crushed, by steps.

A grey cat slips beneath the bushes.
Birds cut into sight.

Last night, I looked at rows of pants, not mine,
but I was wearing blue suede boots and a worn red tee.

Maybe it was the water from the spring: the test they said,
said *toxic,* the spigot erect from the stone, clear as a catheter.

Bad stomach, I dream of dragging up, by rope, quiet white children,
up a hill that is familiar,

many legs pushing up to the top,
where I look down at more mist. The mountains,

thick with smoke, undone by what mist that coats
the top of the trees framing the centered sun.

48. LUCY, AWAY

Tonight, my home, a shroud in blackness. My gut breaks down parasites
that ingest what they devour.

I am tired of being surrounded by the noise of their gesticulations. Often,
the sky opens up into a hole beyond the trees

where I share the blues. What I see is the way I saw the black as I asked him:
"Are you normally a late sleeper?" I hated him,

and did not even realize this, but I tried to move, until I fell forward,
spinning: I love my legs, which are long and slender.

I love my height, which leads me to the point where I am
never pulled back. I love the way he wants to please.

The way he looks into the grey matter of my sky,
burning out the faces of some others he recognizes. He likes me.

I know he likes me, but wants not to say what he feels,
like a dealer on a corner, who drops his hands, pounds, or whatever

they say. I say there's a screen, and I am shooting it through myself,
compressed voice, condensed body reeling against what there is,

a great light which sets above my ground, I look out into
night's draw—

It was a feeling I sensed, someone coming up from behind me,
my skull, hammered open.

49. LUCY, THE GREY CAT, AND SENSE

"Shit." This is what the white trash cleaning woman says before she downs
her coffee to fuel the rest of her day, a day I could never live through.

I'm too fine. There's no way in hell that I'd let my hair get that flat, streaked
sans intention. White Shorts? Pleats? And there's no way I'd grow a gut.

There's Lipo. There's reason, which is best suited to my doing so many lifts that my body is
one line that leads to the sun. There's also my soul, which is transcendent.

I breathe in the air, here, up high, despite the mist that comes down as one surface,
making it so hard for me to breathe in deeply the smell of anything else.

In the morning, I saw the grey cat again. At first, in my periphery, funny,
I read it as, *skunk*, the streak looking more black on white, than white on grey.

Which is a matter of distinction. Like sometimes, when the dew is so thick on the grass,
I have to walk like I am walking on the moon to get to my delicates

out on the line. This morning I said: "you look nice and white," to someone else who
was not white, but was wearing white.

I thought that this was enough. Would I think this of his shadow, then?
Would I think, he's black, and not wearing black, or he's green, walking up a green hill?

I can feel her coming—my room cannot wait. White maid. Black mule, pulling children
up an endless hill, roped by the steel tail I misread as there, not there, there.

In the gills of a fish, the venom pulses. In the body, I sense her coming, and what would
this do for my eyes, the yellow streak, scales bleeding into the blue?

No stars shine out in a white sky. My realization is not like me walking over the grass,
nor like the steps that I might make, lumbering through the clover, *I do try.*

50. LUCY AND THE PHENOMENA

Today, I let a fly go. The fly was slow, dumb and brown with orange stripes.
It was stupid, like the Wood-Pile, or like me, talking.

Why didn't I stop? What made me argue so hard for the dumb, mute,
who spit on four signs behind a row of fences?

In the night hour, when I am cornered up a wall, my face glued to the edge
of nothing to say of my insecurity, a lock, the fog rips me out of sleep.

Or in the night, when I see a fat black, running near the edge of a pillar,
and leaping, the slow motion breaks matter, a ramp of speed: this is the latch.

Two big black pieces of flesh that fall down to the edge of my screen, where
it should be empty: This fog is so thick. "...an early start..." "...I've been at it forever..."

My eyes let in more mist, out of the deepest sleep I've had for so long.
I ran up a great hill, where I fell into a trance. In this body, my own force:

There are rivulets, open in me, but today I think about how I
Let the black fly in. Slowing outside my window,

there's a car. It's silver, and its back is clean, without blemish.
My body is pushing, with my spine opening.

In the white of my skin, dusted to the most delicate yellow,
a white flashes out across a wire that snaps out over a well,

where the spigot is pushed, still, into stone. You will find me there,
waiting with my eyes glued to where I might ask you to not trespass.

51. LUCY, HER RIVER AND SKY

The current let me swim up against the waterfall, until the edge of it swept me out
over the rocks into an eddy, where I shut my eyes.

I did not imagine leeches, sticking to my body. In fact, I thought of the sun, a bright spot
in the gray field I snapped a shot of before I left home.

I am waiting, here, at the edge of the river's shore, staring from under my own blood,
with my eyes shut until the red reels behind them.

A sea sheen shoots across the sky, and I vacate to clear across space.
I am useless.

I am less than the rock I am laying on, less than moss, green and unseen but I feel flat and
secure after falling in its rush.

Out of the river, up on a rock, the forest is invisible, because I am lost in the middle of it.
I unwind to nothing.

Sometimes, my body floats out of control, but here on a ledge, where the water pushes
out over me into more water, I can breathe.

There is no one to see this. There is none, but an edge of rock. I am here, un-named, un-
object, lying.

In the air, I look up at a line between what I see—my sky—and what I can't the inside of my
eyelids lit with an orange I've not seen this bright.

Staring into it on my back, floating in the current, I look up into what my sight, splits.
Here: who would I say I am?

I am not like the water, flat and brown. I am not liquid, fish, or to be read as anything but
human.

My fat back keeps me surfaced, unturned over. I float. My arms spread out to keep me still.
I know there is a black on the shore, his gut, earthed in by muscle.

Unmarked: Am I white, here, out at the dead edge of flow?
My body lost and no-one to call me: anything.

52. LUCY, DISSED

I'm far from the water, far from my head, my gray mane
a frizzy whisper (even if under glass) I'd not be labbed.

Still defined by size, though, I'm smaller than the Hottentot,
larger than the other Lucy: she's the dark, annoying nightmare.

And I walk at a pace that gets me seen. So when I see him,
wet, down the street, in shorts that smell like the river—

No, I'm not a dog, so I can't smell as deeply—but, he stinks.
His hair, which is not like mine, short and laid to the skull,

holds in his brain. But he's some like me, a mirror, shot
towards what makes me pretend not to look.

I don't say "Hi." In fact, I turn. His brown body is
seared in my white brain. I think he sees the pink inside

of his own lids. It's cold, but I'm hot to find his eyes,
the lock between my milky blues and his cover. I speed,

passing one to see another—"Hi," — I say, might as well
be bat sonar, mapping out my blindness. So cool,

I get ignored, and then I hear it: "You got DISSED!"
Did he say that there, rushing up the stairs, a silence,

that mistake, climbing? Up out of what I think is supposed
to be a clear morning, where me, a white greets, maybe

another, at least in likeness, a framed encasing, caught—
 I choose to look down: my spider veins, matte.

53. LUCY GETS IT

Shadows do matter. I learned about being dumb and white,
which is not like being smart and black.

We watch a squat white man walk away. Each of us, untied
but it's, him, who I want to mount.

I guess getting it is hard, because I'm a woman, and white,
tall and thin, sometimes, weighed down only by what sucks

my shape. And that black, is all muscle and matter, his skull,
a precipice, precious matter, which I am inside, somewhere.

Inside of me is a heart that beats high when I run up hills,
flowing up in a state in which I'd like to be stilled.

There's a sentence I am born into: *I am a woman.*
I am long. I am a shadow. I break through ear-plugs, past

birds, beating air, yet I need to be quiet. I need to not be yelled at.
Ears spring open against this hope.

Where oh where has my heart gone? Where I have lost
myself, vanishing, in the numb of my ever known body—

54. LUCY'S HEART WILL NOT STOP

In the mountains, I feel safe, where the pavement is black,
below my feet. If I painted, I would stop to stare.

Three of us here: one short, in tight acrylic,
a second in where a pool sits against a hill. Fat,

the third, a pipe that's rusted out, through wood, struck up
in the swell. In what I have reached, a caw in the present

tense, as in *crow*: A black fist opens up to flight. Fingers,
what more can I do but to hurl myself?

As in the snail's death found on the road, and in its shell
crushed, the life of the two white horses below

me today, in the dirt road. I close my eyes against
sleepiness, I am waiting at the side

of the road, no signal for a call, only the weight, my body
still a current, below some sea bar, past a reef—it, too, pulls.

55. LUCY SEES FLEETING SIGNS

In a grid, through the screen, a small hole, torn. Through it, a green yard behind my house
I cared about this morning.

However, I could care less about the shadows that fall at dusk across the thick field
below my window, the black carpet, light and shadow, tree, blocking sun.

When I see a woman, who looks nothing like me, walking across my line, I don't think
those are her black pants kicking in the wind. I think, instead, the trees blow free.

I look at the side of a house with one window pushed up against a lever that restricts clarity
—out of this exhaustion, my foot, pressed, asleep.

I want, so bad, to be free, to run across the space. A top spun in the brain, I free myself
of time and place.

Such is my back, which after Advil, is healed. Such is my walking,
where I carry my clothes back to dry.

In the wind, I stare out through the circle that opens a spot on my chest, full of the spigot
from which I'll no longer drink.

Being around no mirrors has changed the way I see my own whiteness, a blank surface
pushed open by drill, chip and sweat. I'm full.

I'm the end of an idea. I turn out. I force a pose to see the flowers that grow
on the side of a field.

Dandelions cut past the ridge. A green map, below that. What am I if only floating
through this hole in the screen?

What blocks the field of my seeing makes me look up, as though forced up in a wind.
My back shocks straight.

There are often holes that I stare through, often shadows that move away. Still, there are wires that hold above me—None snapping. No collapse.

56. LUCY STOPS

I object to the horizon. Unless in it, there's the sun, gleaming out across the matter
of my own consequence.

Metal bits lay out in a circle. When I saw them walking up the hill, I thought about the
furiousness of my voice held in by taped mouth.

It helps to be leaning against a wall, my body weighed down by dull fragments
that push me down a path, where I'm spent.

Here, my earplugs are useless. In the evening, when the crickets scratch the night,
singing in the black, a song of endless and empty sound, I think about throwing.

I toss my dog-stick in the watering hole, which liberates, breaking the current—
a silent dog, its clouded eyes, I pass.

I lay on the rocks, undone, my body bent and spread. My hands, heavy, their weight
pounds down into a void: to see the shift.

57. LUCY, SMUG

If I were you, sitting there, next to the white wall, a black grate latched
into the side of the house, I wouldn't say a thing.

In the forest, a shining tree breaks against the leaves where metaphor fails. It must be
horrid to be a black, tender or solid, fluid-filled or packed.

I follow my instinct to the rocks, in the middle of a river, which winds, wildly across
what I hate, my constant having to ask the spelling of your name.

Near the edge of the mouth of another dumb subject is not the weight of silence,
is not being quiet when I need to—it's that I'm winded.

Fire ignites, flooding the heat of my face until it explodes.
I twist in the room, bake, and peel.

I break a grey block, hard, against a wall. I hate them. I hate him. To think, to be
cornered is like being swallowed whole. In the end, I hate you, too.

In the heat, I'm not burning but find myself, climbing. If I were not me, would I respond
as variously to the ropes of hair, wet and matte on the tile?

Would I listen to the sound of the trees shaking on the mountain? What if I were
as round and useless as a load of fleshy brown fat?

What if I, too, were so slow, so pulled back by the shore, so equal to the freight of feeling,
wound to indecision? Two spiders, dead, under a white table, one a daddy long legs.

One has killed another, leaving its hull under the furniture, sucked dry. Another, dead,
gripped in the shape of a thin lantern, a teeny, tiny jellyfish.

58. LUCY VS. FREE

I will not pace, because my heart endures, nor will I
be shot in the face after knocking. Big on the couch,

in the night, or drunk driving home, petite, elastic, I.
You're step is so hard, the floor shakes, I jettison—

Were you me, and I could have been there,
looking away from death. Somewhere, there is a razor

under a tongue, and I'm ready to blow it out, by cheek,
puffed in my house, there is only me, lost in the memory

of what can't be protected Vs. How I am always read.
I never wondered, *was I a site of labor*? I admit it.

I was never a missing link, either. Shaking chair,
I am not waiting to do anything but to live, unleash,

as hard as my unraveling is, it's still a combo, of fear,
and of my hate, slid under the covers, *out,*

out—As hard as this undoing is, I turn its heft over
to what draws my face to yours, say: "You look, so tired."

59. LUCY CULTIVATES JOY

If I watch the river, where it's clear, no brown, I feel safe. If I listen to my face, again,
cracking, then I'm spun silk, staring through to bottom.

It's always the same, the unforgiving spiral, lead undone by the heat of day,
steel gone to cool. In my own summation, I have to make myself up as I can.

I leap over the walls of my undoing, the unmade bed, burned across the twisted rods
of my enzymes.

Nightmare—alarm, un-done. Movement breaks across the territory of what's caught
in my throat. Sound is no hurdle.

The push of feet, under the banging blinds—what cracks across the edge?
Is there a wire in my open heart?

Bind this: If the heart pounds a matter, cutting into me – there's nothing
between two earplugs, reassessing.

The morning shadows lay flat on the trees, the stripes, slapped where the sun opens up,
cuts into the pine's decay.

In a dream, maybe it was mine, I saw a sniper, who was both shooter and victim,
dressed in off-yellow, standing in the forest, talking with a decoy.

What am I running away from? Would a white think that a body of mine, millioned,
blacked behind bars, would think?

Some day. Some way, no how: insecurity, unlocked. Step forward into my foot.
Maybe you are what they say?

The light is lost against the tree, erased like the clothes snatched off the line. What's left is
nothing stretched out across the poles.

60. LUCY AND LIGHT

My sense tells me the blue will burn through the gray of this morning's matte.
The white clapboard running below the house will chip.

The screen will be shocked by a car's rush, moving air, carrying its weight
along the street, the wind behind.

I've done everything, risen in the morning earlier than the birds.
I've stuffed, again, my ears, shut.

Yesterday, what did I think when I slid the box over with my foot, as pointed
as a ballerina's effortless hiding any muscle in her kick?

To the dark, I owe nothing. In fact, what world I leave behind is a projection
of my own need to not touch anything.

When I've cut off one sense, no other returns in its place, only the sound
of blood, banging behind my ears.

There's no light beyond the sun and the small lamp in the corner of the room,
no light but my own eyes, shining against the opaque.

White against gray, I imagine blue, behind that surface which pushes one color
in front of another—The tree's trunk has a worn, white notch near the center.

This is like my eye, not almond but closer to a slit. No breeze through the skin,
the void sealed by bark bulbous over bark.

61. LUCY, HATER

The sky this morning is clear and endless, as are the clouds before the sun erases them,
as is the time before Mars shows itself.

Often, the end of clarity is like this: this color, its name, or what is written in pencil on
the black of night, dulls.

But what is my hate that spurns through my body, like a weight that never breaks?
In the spell of the deadening hour, a watch curls around a wrist.

In the morning, my hate melts the fish in where I swim.
This body is not thin, despite my leaving it.   Caught

by my sense in the lit hour, *shame*. In the flood,
I am lost. In the shift of currents that break under,

I, held under, *I suck*, into an undoing. To reach under,
to seethe:

What's broken is in my heart, sliding inside my chest,
My hate is unabated. Erase, regenerate—so, too, the spillage of deft speech.

62. LUCY, THE JUST WASHED

My body, such a rag, wet, walking through what I'll never see,
the mark of being meant to be caught.

What I don't have, pictures of me,
only the trace of the edge of the fan that sits on the desk.

Silence staggers across my projection, a white imagination,
black as the absence

of light: so, I was born out of the flash of orange that sears the pines,
then vanishes into my own hair soaked.

Isn't it strange—to court my own life—through another?
Low blow: the speculating self, next to the stilled body.

It was smiling, cheesing and grinning, realizing that—as the subject—
(this, I whispered) was undone by the snapping of a shot, *all mood.*

63. LUCY LEARNS A LESSON

In the end, I am like the minnows darting over the mossed rock,
slick with sun, racing from the body warmed by

the heat burning through the day.
A black, darker than the brown one, wades in the wake.

Sometimes, when my breath is tight, I don't try
to keep my seeing inside. I hold my cramping muscles in,

let them shudder with my own breath. My life is not layered
in fat folds. Okay, some, where my body melts

near the shore—in my own figure, I am reclining.
My hair twists down to two points that hang from my smile,

which does connect though less like the paper clip bent in half
on the table with which I dig into my ears.

The hiss of the kettle shoots out into the day,
Why am I trying so hard to be wanted?

My body tugs: Imbalance. Rejection.
Of course, the sign: air under the engine, air out of voice,

I know it's in my breath, warm with spit, caked
as I know, some rocks, as in moss, too, grows thick

green by knowing, what did you want to say?
Teeth jumbled up, small and close inside your mouth.

64. THE OPENING LUCY SEES

In the sky, next to the house, slats of olive show.
Soon, I'll leave here, and someone else will be staring.

Soon, a body will sing, marked, inside the drill of song.
The sky is pink, and against my skin, I blend in to escape.

At night, my body feels like an edge, the tip of a spinning top,
dropped to the sound of what muffles in my ear.

Sure, the hum, which binds me, tight, I pull across the lake,
the one I made up, wide and clear, stretching beyond my sight.

I stare, quickly, up the side of a house, where I shift
into pieces of a self, which is not shattering,

but still falling out of myself, and releasing through my back, I leak,
where I am making a mirror of the sky,

capturing one thing after the next, then hurling them up.
In this flash, my own reply—

Alert: Shadows in the hull of my undoing, finding their way
across more than what's revealed. Often, I choose to run.

I am not going to fake it. I am not going to pretend that I
do not exist beyond the slow darkening of a less pink sky

—someone else's, in a picture even. I am a lever of race
that shoots back out of who I am, even if I wait for the sound

of myself to unlatch from the clutch,
isn't there a shadow, here, that can bring me to?

65. LUCY LOOKS

I'm not sure what matters anymore, especially beyond the grey chair's legs,
stuck in the sun spots, brown, opening in the grass.

I wish I could be more whimsical, or say that the form I have chosen to speak in,
were mine. I am less efficient—

my race is never suspect, because I walk into a room and lay flat
against the walls,

a super sheening against more than anything than the leaves outside,
and there are times when I cannot see, and make dumb comments

of what's promised in the under-painting, like it might be in the tree's matter,
or frozen under the silence of my attention to what's revealed.

I know people are chattering, in their sleep, about my face, my body,
what I did wrong.

What am I saying in the morning,
when I am barely clear?—when what I am saying

in the afternoon, beats down on my back,
the buzz of the hour in which I paint my eyes black.

66. LUCY LEAVES

In the morning, when the sky is still grey, I don't think about seeing another who will not look like me.

I do not think about the way the eyes float through the surface of my mind, a field, brimming with white shadows, dropping down through the sky to take hold of my step.

It hits the pavement, lightly, like salt dropped in the hand, or after the salt has been shook on the plate.   But I am not so silent.   Even when I want to be full, I cannot.

Even when I want to walk miles from my home, up the hill, stopping at the point, where the sky burns into the surface of the water, I can't see

more than the layers of light which pocket in the trees, illuminating the start of the forest, where the trees bind their backs into the sky.

Between me, and the leaves, there are miles, but where I walk, the forest is paved over as if in a habit I've developed from being seen, everywhere, and come

to think of it, I've never thought of myself as invisible, a hole, a corner in a room, a lost voice echoing to no-one in a vacuum.

Clusters of leaves hang down over me, the wind shaking the tips that arrow down through my own seeing. For instance, the chair I am looking at is sunless.

There are rows of shadows that sit out in front of me, walking around the zig-zag of my seeing, like leavings of fat from a piece of meat that I want to bury.

There is seeing this, a matter of my own patience. My step is heavy each one dropping slowly, over the paint worn out on the steps to walk where I want.

67. LUCY GETS INTO THE MIST

I didn't think it was rain. Besides, I hung my tank out to dry, and the idea of slipping on something wet wasn't a possibility. The window seemed to bubble between leaves.

I was a girl, fat. My eyes opened up to the sky, and what I saw was the moon, cut across by the light of delirium in a field.

I was swinging, back and forth, moving as though my very life was floating through my swinging. I was hovering above the bark of the playground, the world below my feet.

I rose and fell from the pendulum. Why did that little brown boy, who was so cute and round pick up the flat basketball and hurl it at my face?

What rage shot through his body—wasn't I his friend? Wasn't I smiling with him in an endless joy, so much so, that my face didn't deserve to be smacked by the ball?

It's morning, and out of the corner of my eye, an orange shadow, the smell of coffee, filling the face of his force, like the discovery of a bungee cord, a black jeep, attacks.

There is my feeling, in remembering, a phantom smack breaking on my face,
the welt of this memory enclosing me deeper in.

68. LUCY LETS IN THE LIGHT

Form for me is a matter of not ripping open the blinds,
or looking through the slats that block the tree.

Green, I should care less about the whole of what I think
and invest in more of what's left behind in shadows,

recessed in the space, I realize, here, there is no-one
like me, my heart still in my chest, yet a feeling of deadness

reached out and tugged across where I am staring through it.
Often, like this, I am stuck not by purpose, but by a kind

of laziness, a feeling that slits into me like an envelope
ripped at one end to let in air. There are lines that come,

and, too, my body sifts across the mark of my own confidence.
I push myself forward, hard, enough to never stop.

There is a fold in my chest, but I remember a fire burning,
and somewhere, I am sweating.

Wild, I don't want to see a white girl in black, or hear two
whites whisper about whatever made this or that structure *great*.

What I am doing is yelling out of a window, seeking waterfalls
or cemeteries, plots, places, where the body

affirms a still, stuck, shape in the mind. My nails are growing,
breaking out of the skin, a hard pulling growth,

where I dream I'm in an elevator, which slides open, a fly
flies up to hit my arm, bounces and takes back off.

69. LUCY AND LOSS

Up a hill, I was going nowhere, so too, the detail not on my eyes, today, the undone face,
twisted in a heart of found rage, some loss, my artifact: a siren screams.

Sometimes, when the sun has no face, I see the back of a white,
buffed by night, a trail of leaves covering my hate for you. In the eyes,

a swipe of my own hate racked and left out, where flowers grow
up through the dirt, and then get walked over, by anyone.

In this way, I see, *waste*. This is the way, too, I see the broken glass on a rock,
pieces that I scrape up and throw out of the earth. Ripped by the pills I take

down to the pool, the interrupted meter of my own making—
sadness cuts into some other white, who actually thinks race is not fake.

What a way to be cooked. What a way to break open the morning,
as the sun rips out over the edge of the mountains.

70. LUCY, FINALLY

I'm sitting here, looking at a shadow, on a wall, looking at a bug, sealed beneath the shower curtain, sitting next to a radiator, burning close.

I'm sitting next to being ignored, as I try to etch out my age,
the light crags flirting with my face.

I'm sitting next to the space in which I am occupying space, where my heart is no longer snagged. I'm sitting next to the wall, where I am engaged,

where I am looking in a mirror, hear the sneeze rings, and I'm feeling kind of iffy,
and what I realize is that I do not like the way that another

who is like me, an object, lit by the light of the morning, looks over my shoulder.
There is one of us, a buffed in black, a white short-sleeved in the forest,

who is walking through an entrenched notion, dumb. I have a surface. I have a spine.
Too, I have a way of being out of which my body springs through the walls.

"I can't help you."— "Sorry don't touch this."—Sorry the night is complicated, even
in the way I run, too—the cardio blast up the hill, says, "You, too, can look like this."

71. REALIZING LUCY

At the top of the hill, before the light gives way to the pine that fractures across the sky,
and the farmhouse, opens its door to shadow, there is a signal.

It is not the dead bird, lying out flat and face down in the middle of the street, its brown
belly on the pavement, cooled by the wind.

It is not in my chest, which opens up into sections as I breathe in the air that almost shocks
me into falling face down as I climb the hill.

It is not the breath. It is not the sky, which I haven't looked at, staring up at the mountains,
which spreads down through the range up the curve.

It is not my knee, which seems at any moment will collapse into if nothing else,
the breaking beneath my legs, the final moment I push up, towards the end of the light.

There are shadows which cover the sign: SUN, painted in blue at the peak of the hill.
So, where, today, will I direct my anger?

Where will I turn, running past the women, who hover up the road, no cars,
crawling into their beers in the middle of the day?

Fat and White. I refuse to grow any fatter, or to not tan. This summer,
I burn off another self, sprinting up the high hill of my own making,

burning Kcals toward the peak of my own release. In this face, "What a view?"—
someone asking another. Was I supposed to seek something else in which to slip?

72. LUCY IS MINE

The way race works, the word, the box, carving through bone.
Contrary to popular belief, it does not box in, rather, it

feels dry. The body that I owned is unfit, soiled with such little
movement that doesn't give.

The smoldering of fireflies in my cup, soiled with sludge:
A memory. A box—you are sitting on top of a box,

remembered, fixed, unfixed: if you don't like it, make it up.
A flat bed truck in which there's a drip, in a room, up a hill,

where I've never been. In it, I'll find my face, which is plastered
to black, an organ, undone—my eyes, a brown, sight—breath, a wish.

Out, across the black road, the burn of pavement, laid across tile.
There is nothing inside of my heart today, but a slow burn

of hatred, where I cut off one voice from another, a spit of sand.
What I don't know is that there is a way into this: I am made up, white.

I, too, am sad. I, too, am a shape. I can't pin me down, except
for what burrows up growing wet in the morning,

hold me back, and if I do not stare for longer than a second—
Dough face: a stupid, flat object will make the body bloat, living.

I've decided to turn in, to arrest and to pull back. I am a given.
I've decided to let go, to hold on to the body, mine, all together.

ACKNOWLEDGEMENTS:

First, many thanks to the Vermont Studio Center, where during a month long residency in 2003, these poems were first rendered; and for the additional gifts of time and resources to ponder, revise and shape this collection over the many years that followed, working and playing at several institutions and residencies, including The CUNY Graduate Center, Mount Holyoke College, University of California, Santa Cruz, The Fine Arts Work Center in Provincetown, The Anderson Center of the Arts, The Headlands Center for The Arts, and The Center for Art and Thought (CA + T).

Enduring gratitude also to these public venues that have supported *Lucy 72* readings and mixed media performances: the Pulitzer Arts Foundation, Fort Gondo Compound for the Arts, California College of the Arts (Cal Arts), Rollins College, Cornell Fine Arts Museum, Stetson University, Atlantic Center for the Arts, The University of Arizona Museum of Art, Conrad Wilde Gallery, POG! Poetry in Action, The Segue Foundation, and The Poetry Project.

I am also forever grateful to the generous friends and colleagues who have engaged with these poems, sharing lasting insight and depth of conversation, namely: Wesley Yu, Erica Hunt, Patricia Spears Jones, Tonya Foster, Dawn Lundy Martin, Duriel E. Harris, Akilah Oliver, Samuel Ace, Farid Matuk, Joshua Marie Wilkinson, Tisa Bryant, Douglas Kearney, Angel Dominguez, especially giovanni singleton, who was the first to publish the earliest of these poems, and to Cornelius Eady, whose brilliant *Brutal Imagination* continues to inspire and activate.

Deepest thanks and love to my dear editors and allies, Sandra Doller and Ben Doller of 1913 Press, who have both supported this work by way of care and grace in publication, design, and in providing various and invaluable performance spaces and collaborations.

Finally, I am and have been humbled, over the years, by the following journals, anthologies, and online platforms that have given the following poems—some in earlier versions—their first light of publication:

"67. Lucy Gets into the Mist," Reprinted for the Creative Writing Program at Reed College. Design and letterpress printing by Letra Chueca Press in Portland, September 2017.

"69. Lucy and Loss," Broadside. *Woodland Pattern Book Center*, March 25, 2017.

"53. Lucy Gets It," "54. Lucy's Heart Will Not Stop," "62. Lucy The Just Washed," *Obsidian: Literature & Arts in the African Diaspora*. Special 20th Anniversary Cave Canem Issue, Fall 2017.

"12. Lucy: Seeing Myself," "34. Lucy, Again, Opening," "46. Lucy Sings," "48. Lucy, Away," "52. Lucy, Dissed," "58. Lucy Vs. Free," *DREGINALD,* Issue 10, Fall 2016. http://dreginald.com/index.php/issues/issue-ten/ronaldo-v-wilson/

"61. Lucy, Hater," "63. Lucy Learns a Lesson," *the Shade Journal*, Volume 1, Fall 2016. http://www.theshadejournal.com/single-post/2016/09/29/TWO-POEMS-by-Ronaldo-V-Wilson

"47. Lucy and Shadow," "49. Lucy, The Grey Cat, and Sense," "65. Lucy Looks," "67. Lucy Gets into the Mist," "68. Lucy Lets in the Light," "69. Lucy and Loss," *Oversound,* Issue 2, Spring 2016. http://www.oversoundpoetry.com/ronaldo-v-wilson-six-poems/

"64. The Opening Lucy Sees," "66. Lucy Leaves," "72. Lucy is Mine," *C.O.U.P.* Special Issue on Privilege, Issue 1.2, Spring 2016.

"71. Realizing Lucy," *Academy of American Poets: Poem-A-Day*, February 15, 2016. https://www.poets.org/poetsorg/poem/71-realizing-lucy

"43. Lucy Sees Again," "44. Lucy, Lucy, Lucy," "50. Lucy and the Phenomena," *"Three from Lucy 72," Fanzine,* January 1, 2016. http://thefanzine.com/three-from-lucy-72/

"70. Lucy, Finally," *BAX Best American Experimental Writing.* Ed. Douglas Kearney, (Wesleyan, CT: Wesleyan University Press, 2016).

"51. Lucy, Her River and Sky," *What I Say: Innovative Poetry by Black Writers in America*, Eds. Aldon Lynn Neilson and Lauri Ramey, (Tuscaloosa, AL: The University of Alabama Press, 2015.

"23. In Lucy," "24. Lucy's Pace," "28. Lucy as Lycidas," "29. Lucy, Again, With Lycidas," "31. Lucy, Where," "32. Lucy is Hungry," "33. Lucy Opens Her Heart," "35. Lucy, The Confined," "37. Lucy Breaks," "38. Lucy Running from Whiteness," "41. Lucy is Not Insane," *Puerto Del Sol: A Journal of New Literature*, Eds. Carmen Giménez Smith and Lily Hoang, Vol. 50, Fall 2015.

"7. Lucy is White," "8. Lucy Responds to Motion and Reflection," "9. Lucy and Redemption," "13. Lucy, The Rain," "17. Lucy and Freedom," *The Volta Book of Poets*, Ed. Joshua Marie Wilkinson. (San Francisco, CA & Portland, OR: Sidebrow Books, 2014).

"25. Lucy and the Sun," "27. Lucy and Movement," "40. Lucy Consumes with Intent," Center for Art & Thought (CA + T) January 15, 2014. http://centerforartandthought.org/work/project/artist-in-residence?page=2

"26. Lucy in a Force," "39. Lucy and her Reality," "42. Lucy's Color," *Provincetown Arts*, (Annual Issue), 2014, 130.

"6. Lucy at the Center of the Universe," "10. Lucy and Violets," "11. Lucy Sees Another Sign," "14. Lucy Almost Drowns," "15. Lucy and Blackness," "16. Lucy Looks," "18. Lucy and Life," "19. Lucy Wakes," "20. Lucy Drowns in Sorrow," "21. Lucy Looks Up at the Great Sky," "22. Lucy's Truth," from Lucy 72, *Bombay Gin Journal*, Naropa University. Iss, 38 Vol. 1. Spring 2014, 103-113.

"1. Lucy Begins to Speak," "2. Lucy Embodies Her Own Practice," "3. Lucy and Regret," "4. Lucy in the Morning," "5. Lucy Tells," from Lucy 72. *EDNA: A Journal of the Millay Colony for the Arts.* Issue 4: 2013. 75-79. http://issuu.com/millaycolony/docs/edna_4_millay_colony_for_the_arts

"36. Lucy, in a Line," "30. Lucy and the Black Wheelbarrow," "55. Lucy Sees Fleeting Signs," "56. Lucy Stops," "57. Lucy, Smug," "59. Lucy Cultivates Joy," "60. Lucy and Light," *InDigest Broadsides from Ronaldo V. Wilson's Lucy 72, InDigest Magazine*, no. 17, August 2010. http://indigestmag.com/blog/?p=4468#.WLyhoktbz1p

"45. Lucy at the Precipice," "51. Lucy, Her River and Sky," *Nocturnes 3 (Re)view of the Literary Arts*, Spring 2004, 40-41.

CONVERSATION | BIOGRAPHY

RVW: I want to say something about the mask as a form, surrounded by the self, a forced vestige, or the only route back through the self, a way of seeing a way back to reality.

LUCY: As someone performing in me, and drawing yourself, how are you getting at a lost lineage, or a broken one? How does the work of recovery perform a way back into necessary encounter?

RVW: Shapes equal language, mark being able to communicate something that makes less sense in accessible language, helping me, through you, to move outside of what we perceive.

LUCY: In all the fabrics, and all of the surfaces that you render—you are learning, a language, in fact, that is familiar.

RVW: Who are you, then, when you, through me, I try? See that PVC pipe over there, black. This is what I mean. Seeing has to do with all of the ways in which there is something impossible—

LUCY: In another time, I will attempt to draw, but for now, I'll be wearing a mask. I will lean my body between the camera and two walls, one, moveable, on wheels, difficult even for you:

RONALDO V. WILSON, PHD, is the author of three previous collections, *Narrative of the Life of the Brown Boy and the White Man*, *Poems of the Black Object*, and *Farther Traveler: Poetry, Prose, Other*. The recipient of fellowships from Cave Canem, the Djerassi Resident Artists Program, the Ford Foundation, Kundiman, MacDowell, the National Research Council, the Provincetown Fine Arts Work Center, the Center for Art and Thought, and Yaddo, Wilson is a mixed media artist, dancer and performer. RVW has performed in multiple venues—as LUCY— at the Pulitzer Arts Foundation, the Atlantic Center for the Arts, Lousiana State University's Digital Media Center Theater, Portland Institute for Contemporary Art, Reed College, CalArts, Cornell Fine Arts Museum, Tube Factory artspace, University of Pittsburgh's Center for African American Poetry and Poetics, and Southern Exposure Gallery. Wilson is Associate Professor of Creative Writing and Literature at the University of California, Santa Cruz.

Titles from 1913 Press:

Lucy 72 by Ronaldo V. Wilson
On Some HispanoLuso Miniaturists by Mark Faunlagui (selected by Ruth Ellen Kocher)
x/she: stardraped by Laura Vena (2017, selected by John Keene)
Umbilical Hospital by Vi Khi Nao
Dreaming of Ramadi in Detroit by Aisha Sabatini Sloan (selected by Maggie Nelson)
Playing Monster :: Seiche by Diana Arterian (Editrixes' Pick)
A Turkish Dictionary by Andrew Wessels (2017, Editrixes' Pick)
More Plays On Please by Chet Weiner (2016, Assless Chaps)
Gray Market by Krystal Languell (2016)
I, Too, Dislike It by Mia You (2016, Editrice's Pick)
Arcane Rituals from the Future by Leif Haven (2016, selected by Claudia Rankine)
Unlikely Conditions by Cynthia Arrieu-King & Hillary Gravendyk (2016)
Abra by Amaranth Borsuk & Kate Durbin (2016)
Pomme & Granite by Sarah Riggs (2015)
Untimely Death is Driven Out Beyond the Horizon by Brenda Iijima (2015)
Full Moon Hawk Application by CA Conrad (2014, Assless Chaps)
Big House/Disclosure by Mendi & Keith Obadike (2014)
Four Electric Ghosts by Mendi & Keith Obadike (2014)
O Human Microphone by Scott McFarland (2014, selected by Rae Armantrout)
Kala Pani by Monica Mody (2013)
Bravura Cool bu Jane Lewty (2012, selected by Fanny Howe)
The Transfer Tree by Karena Youtz (2012)
Conversities by Dan Beachy-Quick & Srikanth Reddy (2012)
Home/Birth: A Poemic by Arielle Greenberg & Rachel Zucker (2011)
Wonderbender by Diane Wald (2011)
Ozalid by Biswamit Dwibedy (2010)
Sightings by Shin Yu Pai (2007)
Seismosis by John Keene & Christopher Stackhouse (2006)
Read 1-6, an annual anthology of inter-translation, Sarah Riggs & Cole Swensen, eds.
1913 a journal of forms, Issues 1-6, Sandra Doller, ed.

Forthcoming:

Conversations Over Stolen Food by Jon Cotner & Andy Fitch
Old Cat Lady: A Love Story in Possibilities by Lily Hoang
Strong Suits, Brad Flis
Hg, the liquid by Ward Tietz

1913 titles are distributed by Small Press Distribution: www.spdbooks.org

L

72